Run to the Rainbow

Modern Curriculum Press
BEGINNING
TO
READ
Series

Library of Congress Cataloging in Publication Data

Hillert, Margaret.
  Run to the rainbow.

  SUMMARY: Three children, searching for the rainbow,
see many colorful objects.
  [1. Rainbow—Fiction]   I. Corey, Barbara.   II. Title.
PZ7.H558Ru   [E]   79-23889
ISBN 0-8136-5065-8 Hardbound
ISBN 0-8136-5565-X Paperback

Library of Congress Catalog Card Number: 79-23889

        4   5   6   7   8   9   10   90 91 92

Run to the Rainbow

Margaret Hillert

Illustrated by Barbara Corey

MODERN CURRICULUM PRESS
Cleveland • Toronto

Oh, look.

Look at that.

Do you see what I see?

Look at it.

Look up, up, up.
Look way up.
How pretty it is!

I see something red.
I see yellow.
I see blue.
I like this.

Look where it goes.
We can go, too.
We can find out where
it goes.
We can run and find it.

Come on now.
Out, out, out.
Go, go, go.
This is the way.

10

One, two, three.
Here we go.
Run, run, run.
This is fun.

12

I see it.

I see it.

Look at that.

Do you see that?

Come on.

Oh, come on.

Oh, no!
That is not it.
See what it is.
That is not it.

14

I guess we will have
to go on.
We will look, look, look.
Now what is that?
What do you see?

This looks good.
It is pretty.
Mother likes it, but
it is not what we want.

17

Come on. Come on.
Run, run, run.
I see something.
Something looks like it.

Is this it?

Is this it down here?

No, I guess not.

Not this. Not this.

Cars make this.

21

Here we go.
Away, away.
We will find it.
See that. See that.

23

Oh, this looks like it,
but it is not the big one.
It is a little one.

24

And I can make a little
one, too.
Look what I can do.
Do you like this little one?

Now where can we go?

What is that?

I see something.

Run, run, run.

27

Oh, look here.
Look here.
Something for us to eat.
Something good, good, good.

We did not find it.
We did not find the big one.
I guess we can not
go where it is.

Here it is.
Oh, here it is.
Come, look here.

No, this is not it,
but it looks like it.
It is pretty,
and it is here where we are.
This is good.

Margaret Hillert, author and poet, has written many books for young readers. She is a former first-grade teacher and lives in Birmingham, Michigan.

Run to the Rainbow uses the 62 words listed below.

a	find	make	that
and	for	mother	the
are	fun		this
at		no	three
away	go	not	to
	goes	now	too
big	good		two
blue	guess	oh	
but		on	up
	have	one	us
can	here	out	
come	how		want
cars		pretty	way
	I		we
did	is	red	what
do	it	run	where
down			will
	like	see	
eat	little	something	yellow
	look(s)		you